With special thanks to the photographers
whose contribution of images made this book possible...

ANDY BROWN   www.envioustime.co.uk
JAMIE QUINN   www.jamie-quinn.com
KAREN WILLIAMS   www.eFestivals.co.uk

First published in Great Britain in 2006
by Artnik
341b Queenstown Road
London SW8 4LH
UK

© Artnik 2006

ISBN 1-905382-31-6

Design: Supriya Sahai
Book Concept: Nicholas Artsrunik
Editor: John McVicar

Printed and bound in Croatia
by HG–Consulting

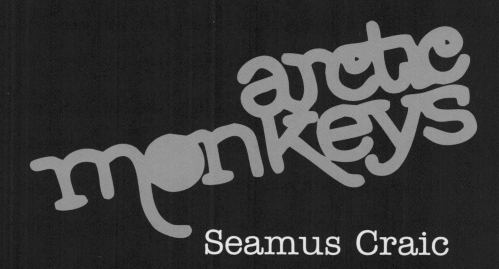

Seamus Craic

artnik books

word 'phenomenon' is one that is bandied about all too often in music when a new band arrives and storms into the top spot. More often than, especially in recent years, the so-called storming is not what it seems. As record sales plummet year after year, with the increasing recourse to dowloading from and sharing files on the internet, the numbers needed to make an album Number 1 are less and less. This puts into perspective all those bands that have appeared on the covers of **NME**, **Melody Maker**, **Q** and so on with their hyped-up 'best-selling' albums.

Bands like Coldplay or the White Stripes, two sharply contrasting bands with dedicated fanbases, are not known for having broken any records, for instance, and are certainly not seen as being part of a wider movement. Yes, they've sold a lot of records but do they represent anyone? The answer to that is probably just record buyers.

It's safe to say that the last true musical phenomenon in the UK was Oasis. They released a classic album in the shape of **Definitely Maybe** in 1994, a powerful collection of songs with some truly irresistible tunes – until recently, the fastest selling debut album of all time. They were to top even that the next year, with **What's The Story, Morning Glory?**, complete with one of the most covered songs in recent years, 'Wonderwall'. The curious thing about this album is that it received a very lukewarm set of reviews, the music press

seemingly reluctant to bestow any more accolades on the cheeky, not to say rowdy Gallagher brothers. Regardless of that, hordes of people went out to buy the album. **What's The Story...** became one of the most potent symbols of the lad culture and it was one of those examples where word of mouth becomes the driving force behind a band's success.

The album's sales eventually outstripped those of **Definitely Maybe** and there were major concerts, such as the giant event at Knebworth (one of the biggest concerts this country has ever seen) which were reflections of the overwhelming popularity of a band: in those days, it seemed that nearly everyone was talking about Oasis, or humming 'Wonderwall'.

Ten years later, another phenomenon has arrived in the shape of the Arctic Monkeys who are even more of a word-of-mouth sensation, a band whose success has been even more meteoric than that of Oasis:

HAVING NOT EVEN RELEASED AN ALBUM BEFORE, SEEMINGLY, EVERYONE WAS TALKING ABOUT THEM!

They are a band whose success has had industry commentators scratching their heads after predicting the demise of the CD market: they may even just be changing the way that music is distributed and consumed.

THIS IS THEIR AMAZING STORY SO FAR

On a catwalk jungle,
Somebody grabbed my arm
A voice spoke so cold it matched the
Weapon in the palm
This is England
This knife of Sheffield steel
This is England
This is how we feel

JOE STRUMMER
THE CLASH CUT THE CRAP

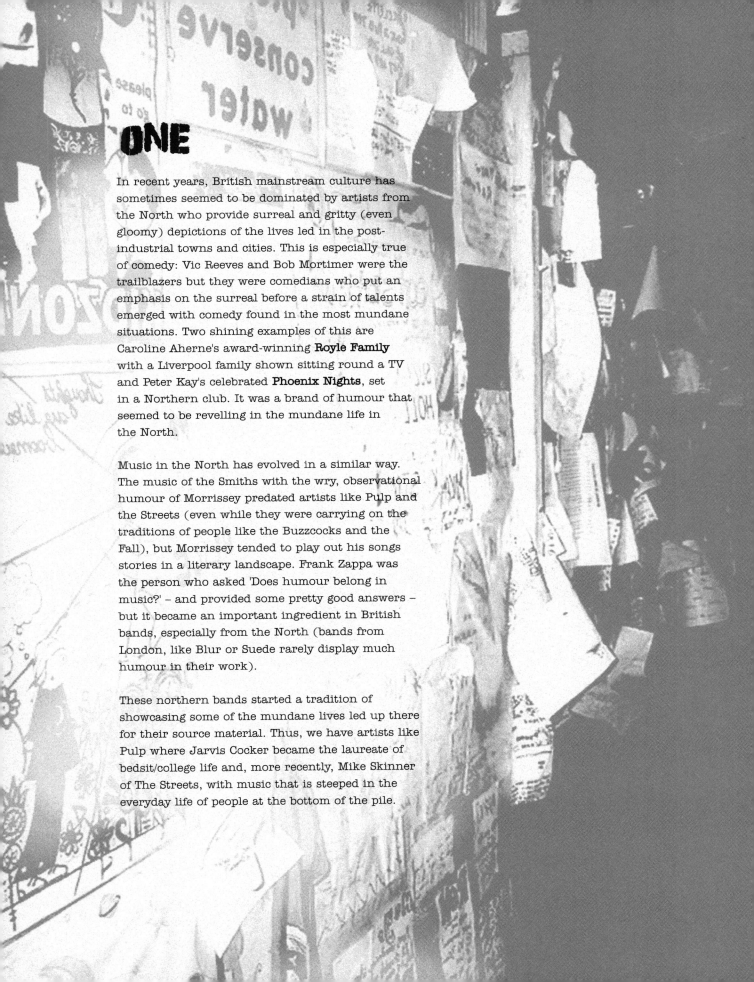

ONE

In recent years, British mainstream culture has sometimes seemed to be dominated by artists from the North who provide surreal and gritty (even gloomy) depictions of the lives led in the post-industrial towns and cities. This is especially true of comedy: Vic Reeves and Bob Mortimer were the trailblazers but they were comedians who put an emphasis on the surreal before a strain of talents emerged with comedy found in the most mundane situations. Two shining examples of this are Caroline Aherne's award-winning **Royle Family** with a Liverpool family shown sitting round a TV and Peter Kay's celebrated **Phoenix Nights**, set in a Northern club. It was a brand of humour that seemed to be revelling in the mundane life in the North.

Music in the North has evolved in a similar way. The music of the Smiths with the wry, observational humour of Morrissey predated artists like Pulp and the Streets (even while they were carrying on the traditions of people like the Buzzcocks and the Fall), but Morrissey tended to play out his songs stories in a literary landscape. Frank Zappa was the person who asked 'Does humour belong in music?' – and provided some pretty good answers – but it became an important ingredient in British bands, especially from the North (bands from London, like Blur or Suede rarely display much humour in their work).

These northern bands started a tradition of showcasing some of the mundane lives led up there for their source material. Thus, we have artists like Pulp where Jarvis Cocker became the laureate of bedsit/college life and, more recently, Mike Skinner of The Streets, with music that is steeped in the everyday life of people at the bottom of the pile.

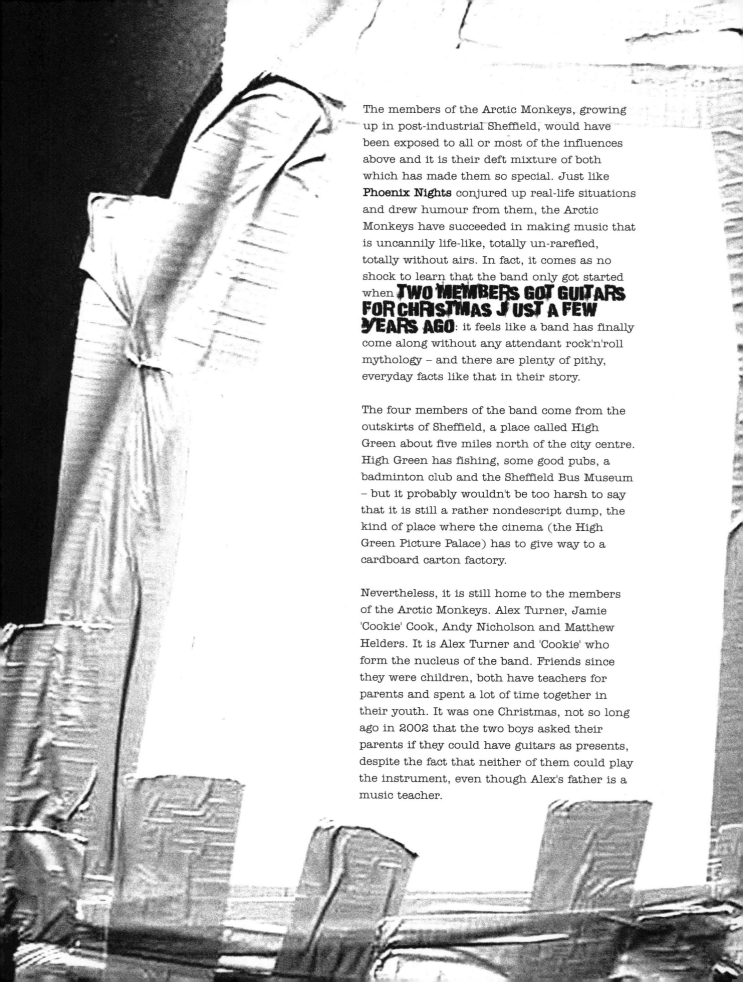

The members of the Arctic Monkeys, growing up in post-industrial Sheffield, would have been exposed to all or most of the influences above and it is their deft mixture of both which has made them so special. Just like **Phoenix Nights** conjured up real-life situations and drew humour from them, the Arctic Monkeys have succeeded in making music that is uncannily life-like, totally un-rarefied, totally without airs. In fact, it comes as no shock to learn that the band only got started when **TWO MEMBERS GOT GUITARS FOR CHRISTMAS JUST A FEW YEARS AGO**: it feels like a band has finally come along without any attendant rock'n'roll mythology – and there are plenty of pithy, everyday facts like that in their story.

The four members of the band come from the outskirts of Sheffield, a place called High Green about five miles north of the city centre. High Green has fishing, some good pubs, a badminton club and the Sheffield Bus Museum – but it probably wouldn't be too harsh to say that it is still a rather nondescript dump, the kind of place where the cinema (the High Green Picture Palace) has to give way to a cardboard carton factory.

Nevertheless, it is still home to the members of the Arctic Monkeys. Alex Turner, Jamie 'Cookie' Cook, Andy Nicholson and Matthew Helders. It is Alex Turner and 'Cookie' who form the nucleus of the band. Friends since they were children, both have teachers for parents and spent a lot of time together in their youth. It was one Christmas, not so long ago in 2002 that the two boys asked their parents if they could have guitars as presents, despite the fact that neither of them could play the instrument, even though Alex's father is a music teacher.

If it seemed like a bit of horseplay on their parts, it hid the serious intention of forming a band. The reason? Because it 'wasn't hard'. Accordingly, they went along to school to find people that could be in this band. They found a bass player, Andy Nicholson, and a 'drummer' in Matthew Helders. In fact, Helders wasn't a drummer at all, he just wanted to be in the band and so as the drumming position was vacant, he went out and got himself a drum kit.

They were all totally normal Sheffield lads, with the only other overriding interest being football. Three of them are Sheffield Wednesday fans, while Cook supports United and plays regularly as well as going to the games (he still plays for his local pub team in a Sheffield Sunday League). Football aside, they were all determined to make something of this band idea.

While all the other members of the band had been persevering on their instrument, Helders (also known as 'The Cat') actually turned up at the first rehearsal using the drum kit for the first time. Alex has recalled: 'when we first got together in the garage, Matt had only just got his drum kit.

'IT'S NOT THAT WE JUST GOT DRUNK, WE JUST DIDN'T REALLY KNOW WHAT WE WERE DOING...

'When we started we didn't really play anything, so playing any kind of music together was an achievement.'

They didn't get carried away, though. They kept everything resolutely low-key by inaugurating rehearsals at a warehouse in Neepsend – the red light district of Sheffield, on an industrial estate near the skate park. They rehearsed in the early evenings and often the moon was coming up as they left for their homes: they would see the drug dealers, the prostitutes and pimps coming out to ply their particular trade. The engineers in the rehearsal rooms would continually give them warnings to be careful and more than a few times they were threatened for money. On the other hand, the skunk was cheap, trippy and on their doorstep

What followed was six months of intensive rehearsals for the band and legend has it that there were dozens of Arctic Monkeys originals that emerged, many of which were ruthlessly purged from the set as they developed a keen sense of perfectionism unusual in such musical novices. Alex was the main songwriter and was developing astonishingly as a lyricist and providing eye-catching titles as they started to build a set for their live debut.

They also needed to have an eye-catching name for the band too, of course, and there are conflicting stories about how this came about. One story had it that that they were named after Dave's uncle's band, another that it was his father's, supposedly known as Arctik Monkeez.

THERE IS ALSO A STORY THAT IT CAME ABOUT THROUGH A MEETING WITH A TRAMP WHO SAW THEM WITH THEIR INSTRUMENTS AND SHOUTED THE NAME OUT.

But since the false story about the tramp appeared on the band's original website, one must doubt that too! Matt Helders put that one in its place in an interview in New York:

'THAT'S A LIE AS WELL. I'LL TELL YOU THE TRUTH. WE MADE THAT UP COS WE GOT SO MANY PEOPLE ASKING US THAT IN THE U.K. EVERY INTERVIEWER ASKED US ABOUT THAT. SO WE JUST STARTED MAKING STORIES UP. WE MADE SO MANY UP THAT IT WAS HARD TO KEEP TRACK.'

The truth according to bassist Andy: 'Jamie were just messing about in class, you know, when you're writing fantasy football teams and band names in the back of your book. He came up with the name. We were about 15 and it all fell into place. We learned to play our instruments and now were here!'

The point is there are no trees in the arctic, which is a bit of a downer if you're a monkey.

Whatsit mean Arctic Monkeys then?
Well they play music that gets the
monkey off your back. As Alex says:
'Come to our gigs and it's normal
working class people having a great
time. That's what music's all about.'

They all had common influences, which
their music gives away, but Alex's main
lyrical inspiration was more obscure
than the Clash, the Smiths, the Jam and
recent artists like System Of A Down and
Queens Of The Stone Age. John Cooper
Clarke, the artist most often
namechecked by Alex, is one of the
unhallowed names of the punk age.

Having started out as a performance
poet in Manchester folk clubs, Clarke
was swept up in the punk phenomenon
and was an opening act for the Sex
Pistols, among others. Tony Wilson,
founder of Factory Records, captured a
fine array of bands at this time on his
legendary Granada programme So It
Goes and here, John Cooper Clarke is
immortalised also. In hyper-realist
'Arctic Monkeys-style' he is shown
handing out tools to students in his dull
stint of work at Manchester University
before performing to a rapt audience

masterpieces such as 'Psycle Sluts',
'Evidently Chicken Town' and 'You'll
Never See A Nipple In The Daily
Express'.

Such titles make the influence on Alex
seem all too clear and he has been
enthusiastic in his praise of Clarke
whom he was to meet later: 'He's this
dead skinny guy with big mad hair, red
tinted glasses and drainpipe jeans, a
proper character. Everyone tells us we've
got a shit band name but he was like
"That's great! There's no trees in the
arctic! How would it survive?" He
painted this picture instantly, a real
creative mind'

Already, thanks to Cooper Clarke, Alex
seemed to have an idea of how he
wanted to come across and was coming
out with some cracking song titles like
'Fake Tales of San Francisco' and 'From
The Ritz To The Rubble'. And the music
they were putting it to was sounding
good too.

**NOW THEY HAD TO GO OUT
AND GET AN AUDIENCE.**

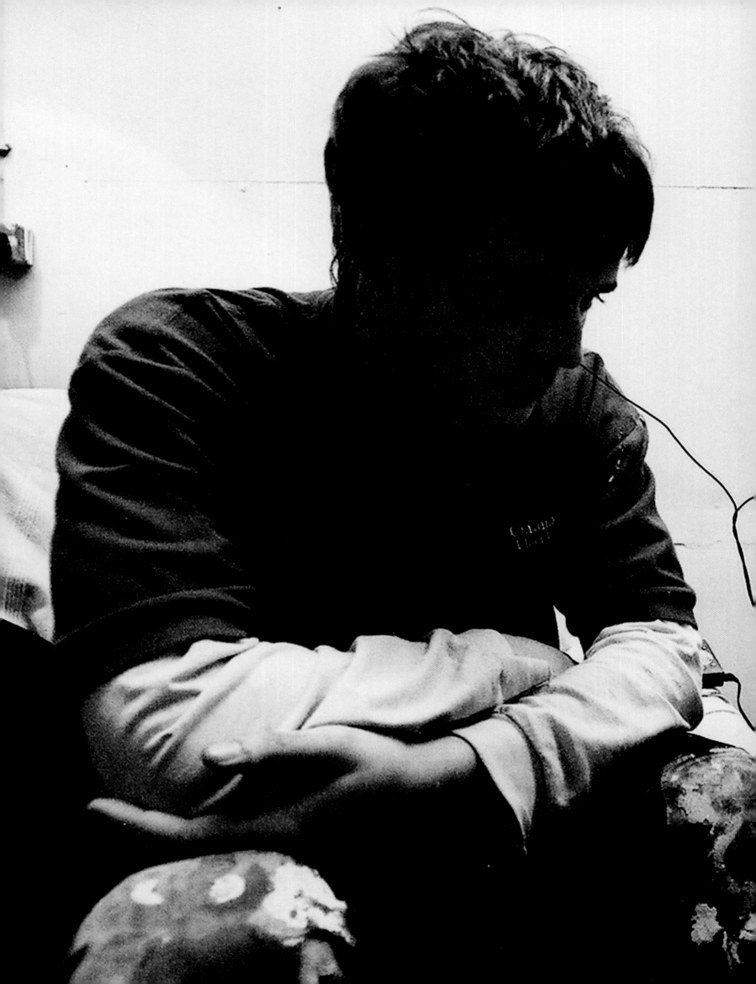

TWO

As in most towns of Sheffield's size, there was always a well-trodden route for aspiring rock stars to go down, and for the Monkeys the first port of call was a pub called the Grapes. Known as 'Sheffield's friendliest live venue', The Grapes is a small place based in the city centre and is a 'good' sounding board for a young band that don't care that much about a professional sound. Perfect, in fact, for a band like the Arctic Monkeys.

The Grapes can barely hold a hundred people and there were certainly fewer there that night when they appeared on a stage for the first time. To their amazement, however, when they came on stage the crowd erupted like George Best had come back in his pomp and elected to play for Sheffield United.

The audience were treated to spiky, but foot-tapping tunes that were played with energy and delivered in a dry, sardonic manner by Alex that spoke to everyone. When they finished their set, the applause was even louder than when they came on. As one London journalist put it later, 'it was

LOCAL 'MUSIC FOR LOCAL PEOPLE.'

It was one of those rare moments where the audience didn't have to try to get what the band were about – the Monkeys spoke to them in words and sounds that were part of their everyday lives.

But was it only that they were a local band for local people? The Monkeys didn't really think so and they were emboldened enough by the reception to carry on and do any gigs that they could get – always by word of mouth and, more importantly, because they were dirt cheap. Around this time, they hit on the idea of recording a demo. Exactly what they were going to do with it, they weren't sure – they just knew they had to have a demo CD. Every new band worth its salt recorded a demo of their best numbers. This is what unknown bands did.

They spent £250 at a local studio and they had a CD with some songs on it: Matt said: 'I think we got more out of that £250 than anyone's got out of £250 before.'

On the back of making at their first gig the grand total of £27, it was a pretty ambitious step to spend this kind of money on a CD, which they hadn't a clue what to do with, and to commit themselves to the making their dream real. At the time, Turner and Helders were thinking about university, Cook was a tiler and Nicholson was on the dole.

So, they had their CDs ready and they were doing some more gigs, popping up in venues all over the north. Usually, a band would now start looking for a prospective manager who might be in the audience somewhere and who could be given a copy, or they could start sending out the CDs to record labels direct.

What happened next was almost like a marketing ploy cooked up by Colonel Tom Parker or Tesco, it was so simple and yet so amazingly productive. Only it wasn't a marketing ploy. Alex said later: 'I used to work in a bar at venues and it really annoyed me when bands would say:

'WE'VE GOT CDs FOR SALE AT THE BACK, THREE POUND EACH.' YOU'D THINK, 'FUCK OFF, WHO DO YOU THINK YOU ARE'.'

It's a familiar scene to people who've been to small-time gigs in recent years. New technology has enabled performers to cheaply produce a CD for their gigs, often complete with makeshift covers, and venues are more than happy to take a cut of the price. In fact, even buskers on the underground flog CDs of their work. Very often, it's a move that backfires on a band because in a lot of cases, people have paid to see the band anyway and they are paying for drinks as well. So, unless they're exceptional, the artist ends up at the back of the gig with a couple of boxes of unsold CDs, having been hoping for a stampede.

So, after an Arctic Monkeys gig, when the band were approached by some people eager to hear them again ('We had this one time where people were literally running up to the stage clambering for these demos'), the band simply handed them over. Though they did it spontaneously and without any hidden agenda, they were totally in tune with current technology.

The advances in music technology make the CD hawkers that fucked off Alex so much like real Luddites. With music file-sharing now so common amongst youngsters, it was only a matter of hours – even minutes – before the new songs that had impressed the Monkeys' audience would be hurtling through cyberspace and then circulating freely. Once they twigged this, they immediately saw that if they were handing out the CD for free they might as well upload it onto the Internet too. One problem was that the Monkeys were not computer savvy: email, iTunes and video games were about it. They hadn't a clue how to design a website.

Matt explains: 'It's not like we had a plan. We used to record demos and then just burn them onto CDs and give them away at gigs. Obviously there weren't many demos available, so people used to share them on the Internet, which was a good way for every to hear it.?

'So we used to share – not us personally, we don't even know how to do it – but fans did. There's a guy who has come along to film us…two guys, actually. One of them is the main guy who put the songs on the Internet. So the fans just used to send them to each other, which didn't bother us because we never made those demos to make money or anything. We were giving them away free anyway – that was a better way for people to hear them. And it made the gigs better, because people knew the words and came and sang along. We can't complain about it.'

Another important job for the band was to make the music 'officially' available on a file sharing website called www.myspace.com, a forum for unsigned bands (of course, the band had to get somebody to do it for them). If it sounds nondescript, then one ought to bear in mind that it was recently purchased by one R.Murdoch and has a lot of cumulative power in its Internet traffic.

In view of all this traffic in their music, perhaps they shouldn't have been surprised – but they were –when things started to happen. They were playing a gig at Wakefield when they came upon a set of hardcore Arctic Monkeys fans – some of whom had driven all the way from Aberdeen. And then there was the gig in Sheffield in Christmas, 2004 that Matt described later: 'It was the first gig where people we didn't recognise were singing along,' he recalled.

'WE WERE LIKE, HOW DO YOU KNOW THE WORDS!!! THAT WAS DEFINITELY THE POINT WHERE WE WERE WONDERING WHAT'S HAPPENING HERE.'

BAD SNEAKERS PROUDLY PRESENTS

ARCTIC MONKEYS

PERFORMING LIVE

MONDAY 17TH OCTOBER

£8 DOORS 7.30PM GRANARY WHARF LEEDS

THE BLANK CANVAS LEEDS

It was the power of the internet that helped in October 2005 make their debut single, 'I Bet That You Look Good On The Dance Floor', No 1 in the UK charts. This came about because a month before Stuart Conroy, 32-year-old boss of Web Warehouse in Cambuslang, Glasgow, build them a website, where they uploaded songs and videos, and had a chatroom.

However, Conroy had to chase the band for his money – their success happened so quickly that bills got neglected.

In November Conroy moaned: 'Now that they've hit the big time, they are refusing to pay the 1400 quid they owe us. This is only the second time we have

been forced to take action against a client who refuses to pay their bills.' It seems that the management of the band only paid the first three weeks the site was up and Conroy was owed another 5 weeks. He has now been paid. Alex said of Conroy:

I KNOW HE'S SCOTTISH BUT HASN'T HE HEARD THAT EXPRESSION 'THE CHEQUE'S IN THE POST'?

When the chatroom first launched around 3,000 fans were logging on to the site each day; by the time they went No 1, it was up to 125,000 hits a day.

The gigs that they were now doing were becoming more and more riotous affairs where the music seemed to inspire, for one thing, a lot of crowd-surfing. Andy later recalled the one in Wakefield:

'We once did a gig in Wakefield and a guy was crowd-surfing and he fell right onto his eye. By the time he got up, he had a black eye but he didn't even care! He did it again five minutes later!'

THIS WAS ALSO THE GIG WHERE VENUE WAS SO 'FUCKING RAMMED' THAT THERE WERE FOOTPRINTS ON THE CEILING LEFT BY CROWDSURFERS.

For all the mayhem, there was a warm-hearted air to proceedings too, with little distance maintained the band and audience...if any. Andy: explained: 'The way we see it, we try not to have a barrier if we can because we don't want to separate the band and the crowd. We want us all

to be one, really, like we've all gone on a journey somewhere. I mean, the only thing that stops Alex singing sometimes is when the crowd-surfing ends up hitting the mike in his teeth. He's already lost a couple of teeth doing that.'

It was all very reminiscent of the fervour last witnessed in the Northern Soul clubs in the seventies, where speed-fuelled revellers would dance ecstatically to obscure soul classics in clubs like the Wigan Casino. But, as the gigs went on and this huge 'secret society' went from strength to strength with the rest of the music world seemingly oblivious to what was going on, a new kind of classic – northern classics – were being honed and perfected.

THREE

The crucial element of the Monkeys' music is pretty obvious: simplicity. These are barely-grown, spotty kids, a couple of whom are only just in their twenties. None of them has had the time or perhaps even the inclination to become experts in their instrument – but they're young anyway and they make up for it by putting huge amounts of energy in what they're playing.

Also, the lyrical themes have a certain tart, minimalist sting, with Alex turning a forensic eye on the people and places that he knows: the drug users, binge drinkers, shabby strangers and disenchanted, unglamorous girlfriends, the street corners, the shops, the dives and the pubs. As he put it himself so evocatively: 'We live in Sheffield and we write about the things we see here. What else is there to write about?'

THOUGH ONLY THE BAND'S PARENTS MIGHT REMEMBER THE ERA POSSIBLY, THE BAND SEEMED TO BE SUMMONING UP A LONG—LOST ERA WITH THESE THEMES—THE 'KITCHEN SINK'.

The 'kitchen sink' era of theatre and films from the late fifties to the sixties is said to have started with John Osbourne's play **Look Back In Anger** and heralded a succession of modern anti-heroes, the 'angry young men' sporting dull jobs and/or girlfriends, thwarted career hopes and often repressed (usually sexual) energy.

It seemed like a cold, metallic energy that was
bursting forth on stage and screen and it was, of
course, one of the precursors to the other age that
the Monkeys were echoing: punk.

It is possible, then, to see the songs as kitchen sink
dramas with a punk backing. The band themselves
would probably be the first to admit that they lack
finesse (it's almost impossible to imagine them doing
a ballad) and the important thing for all the songs
seems to be creating a sense of immediacy.

Classic rock they may not be but it was the perfect, resounding backing to the brilliant tales that Alex told which already had mock-classic status among those in the know. A glance across the titles of the songs that were now being shared showed that he had a quite brilliant way with words, a knack for strong imagery combined with a satirical eye and local vocabulary: 'I Bet You Look Good On The Dancefloor', 'Fake Tales Of San Francisco, 'You Probably Couldn't See For The Lights But You Were Looking Straight At Me', 'Riot Van', 'Red Light Indicates Doors Are Secured', 'From Ritz To The Rubble' and 'Mardy Bum'...

THEY ALL DEMANDED TO BE HEARD.

'I Bet You Look Good On the Dancefloor' is a tightly-paced, infectious stomper about romantic frustration and claustrophobic nightclub rituals, with a sly reference to Romeo and Juliet:
'Oh there int no love no, Montague's or Capulets just banging tunes in DJ sets and
Dirty dancefloors and dreams of naughtiness'

'Fake Tales Of San Francisco' is a biting satire of music industry types who live in a self-deluding dreamworld:
'I'd love to tell you all my problem
You're not from New York City, you're from Rotherham

So get off the bandwagon, and put down the handbook
Get off the bandwagon and put down the handbook'

'Riot Van' is a binge-drinking song, while 'Red Light Indicates Doors Are Secured' ponders, in almost an existential way, the problems of getting large parties into cabs after an evening at a nightclub. Such is the arch humour of Alex, the listener is somehow never oppressed by some of these epics of the humdrum and thick Hovis slices of inconsequence – like the deeply disappointed lovers in 'Mardy Bum':
'Now then Mardy Bum
I see your frown
And it's like looking down the barrel of a gun'

It was all rooted in reality, however glum or trivial – and there was some kind of mad genius at work with a line like this from 'A Certain Romance':

THERE'S ONLY MUSIC, SO THAT THERE'S NEW RINGTONES.'

Very soon, Alex would be compared to Mike Skinner of the
Streets, who also has a way with titles. His 'Today I Have
Achieved Absolutely Nothing' is a trawl through a frustrating
day where, figuratively speaking, Skinner is short-changed by
life while he is trying to change DVDs that he has bought as
well as other inane tasks that drive him round the bend. The
Streets' music is somewhat Skinner-centric and exclusive to him
– the greatest strength of the Monkeys' music and Alex's lyrics
was it was highly inclusive, a series of anthems for bored,
excluded youth.

The punk energies that they were harnessing were all part of a
self-generated movement between them and their audience. But
unlike the earlier punk bands, who had cultural input from
fashion and left-wing politics, the monkeys had nothing. It was
probably because of this that the wider world of music did not
pick up on the street buzz that the Arctic Monkeys were
making. But this was going to change in the spring of 2005
as A&R men began to start hearing reports from clubs about
**THIS UNSIGNED BAND WITH HORDES OF FANS WHO
WERE, SOMEHOW, ALREADY SINGING ALONG TO
THEIR SONGS AT SOLD—OUT GIGS.**

ON MAY 2 2005, THEY RELEASED
THEIR OWN PRODUCT ON A LABEL
CALLED **BANG BANG RECORDS**, WHICH
WAS SAID TO BE ONE OF THE BAND
NAMES THAT THEY REJECTED IN
FAVOUR OF ARCTIC MONKEYS.

Five Minutes with Arctic Monkeys featured the songs 'Fake Tales of San Francisco' and 'From the Ritz to the Rubble'. This release was limited to 1000 CDs and 500 7" records, but was also available to download from the iTunes Music Store. James 'The Sheriff' Sheriff (now webmaster of the band's official website) also put the contents of **Beneath the Boardwalk**, a renamed upload of one of the band's demo CDs – freely available to download from his webpage. These tracks quickly became available on several peer-to-peer file-sharing networks.

They now had an even wider and more enthusiastic fanbase than ever before, many of whom would travel miles to see them play. There was one bunch from Nottingham who would go to every show. 'They turn up with a bag of wine and a straw,' laughed Matt, 'so they can crowd-surf and sip at the same time.'

There was even more of an A&R clamour and, cheekily, many of these A&R men were turned away from the guest-list entrance on the Monkeys' orders – a very rare and undignified experience for an A&R man. The band's attitude was that they'd got this far on their own – why let these people in for free? Of course, this only produced a desperate scramble among the record execs to sign this new band that was playing sell-out gigs purely on word of mouth. The Monkeys had cracked it without airplay or TV or PR, and they didn't suck up to the industry...

THEY HAD TO BE SPECIAL.
THEY WERE GOING TO MAKE SOME
LABEL A LOT OF MONEY.

There was naturally a lot of interest from major labels but in this respect the band were initially in a bit of a quandary. They had already created the kind of excitement that many record companies pay thousands to PR companies to create. Why did they have to go to a big record company just to do that all over again? They knew that they could sell records – they were playing to people nearly every night who were desperate to buy their music. What they were missing, of course, was the organisation needed to sell a record, a distribution network.

Once they realised that they couldn't really go it
alone, they had to listen to offers and some of
them were big: the temptation of money saw
the band almost sign for 'another label' but they
then started to consider a label called Domino.
The band was attracted by Domino owner
Laurence Bell, and the attractions were pretty
obvious: he ran the label from his flat and only
signed bands that he liked personally. It was
also a good move in that one of their label-
mates would be another music sensation of the
year, Franz Ferdinand.

Franz Ferdinand

NICHOLAS ARTSRUNIK

In many ways, Franz Ferdinand were musically a world away from the Arctic Monkeys. They were a band from Glasgow with an art school background and their music was a lot less less frantic than the Monkeys, a measured remoulding of the New York punk sound of bands like Talking Heads and Television. What they had in common, however, was a compulsion to be away from the mainstream in music and both bands tried to studiously ignore the furore that surrounded them: not get sucked into what the Monkeys were starting to call 'the bollocks'. It was essentially a basic 'indie' posture

that both bands had, and it was something that was respected at an independent label like Domino.

Of course, this was again reminiscent of Oasis, and the comparison is illuminating. Oasis were always (and still are) fiercely proud of being part of an 'indie' heritage, signed to Alan McGee's legendary Creation label. It's seldom appreciated that this 'indie' label is, in fact, part of a licensing deal with EMI which was in place from the start: Oasis actually signed to a pseudo-independent label that was just a front for a major.

Even after the Arctic Monkeys signed a deal with Domino, there were still reports that they were courting major labels: much later, the **Daily Star** reported that the Domino deal was followed in October 2005 by a £1m publishing deal with EMI and a £725,000 contract with Epic for the United States. This was strenuously denied, however, on the band's website, which dubbed the paper 'The Daily Stir'.

Matt said of the deal: 'We were ready to sign to a different label. I was tempted by the money on offer because it meant I could give up my day-job. And then Lawrence came to watch us. He seemed like a genuine fan. He decides who he signs, rather than some MD. It all seemed just right, so when the rest of the band met him, we signed to Domino right there.' It all went back to how deals were done in the days of the independent labels of the 70s and early 80s – New Order signed to Factory, and The Smiths to Rough Trade.

And rather than being a 'local band for local people', it seemed clear that the Arctic Monkeys were, in fact, like New Order and the Smiths, a 'people's band'.

NOW ALL THEY NEEDED WAS A HIT SINGLE.

FOUR

The release of their first single, which was to be 'I Bet You Look Good On The Dancefloor', was quickly slotted in for October 2005. Meanwhile, the paper renowned for discovering new young talent, the **NME**, finally bestirred itself to start mentioning the Arctic Monkeys in depth for the first time. Our rock bible's first-ever mention of the band had been a five-line review of a gig in Sheffield in March (there was also a paragraph on them when they supported the Coral in Sheffield in May).

It was the end of May when the **NME** got a profile together of them and they focused mostly on Alex. It was becoming clear that the Monkeys weren't just another group of lads shouting away to some scuzzy four-chord rock'n'roll... their frontman was adding a unique finesse to the band. Alex revealed that he'd been writing for some time but had had a problem letting even his own crew know.

'I've been penning things since school,' he said. 'I've been writing for longer than my friends realise.

YOU COULDN'T BE CREATIVE AT SCHOOL. YOU'D HAVE THE PISS RIPPED OUT OF YOU.

'Even when we started the band, lyrics were an area that we were ashamed to talk about and we just wrote bollocks to start with. But I'd always write things in secret and one day I just thought "Fuck it, I'm gonna do it for real".'

The quality of those lyrics couldn't be disputed either as the **NME** made a note of all the fans that were singing along with Alex, not to mention, as they also noted, carrying him on a sea of hands at their first gig in London.

The fact that Alex and the band were getting their first real mentions in the spring of 2005 (the **NME** called them Britain's Hottest New Band in May) was either a measure of the Monkeys phenomenon, where all the the usual channels for exposure were simply outflanked – or the complacency at the **NME**, who had been seemingly blissfully unaware of a band with no singles or albums that attracted hordes of fans at sell-out gigs and who knew all the words to their songs.

To illustrate the latter, one only has to take note of the **NME** issue a couple of weeks after the live review. With much fanfare, the magazine was giving away a CD featuring the best new bands in Britain. A varied but not uninteresting brew this was, the best known being Bloc Party, Maximo Soundpark and the Kills. But could any of them or any of those on the compilation claim that all the people that came to their gigs were able to sing all the words to all their songs? The **NME** really had missed the Arctic Monkeys boat.

And as this was happening, there was new internet activity going on which raised their profile still further. Before now, the visits to their website had originated from chat rooms and blogs, where excited fans swapped news and impressions of the band.

From about June 2005, search engines became a more important source of visits in June 2005 as the band's name recognition grew. This was now viral marketing on a scale that hadn't really been seen before (For the record, in early 2006, the Arctic Monkeys are not just the most searched-for band on the internet but are also the most popular band online, accounting for 3.25% of visits to the Bands and Artists category in the last week in January – up from 1.89% market share just a week earlier).

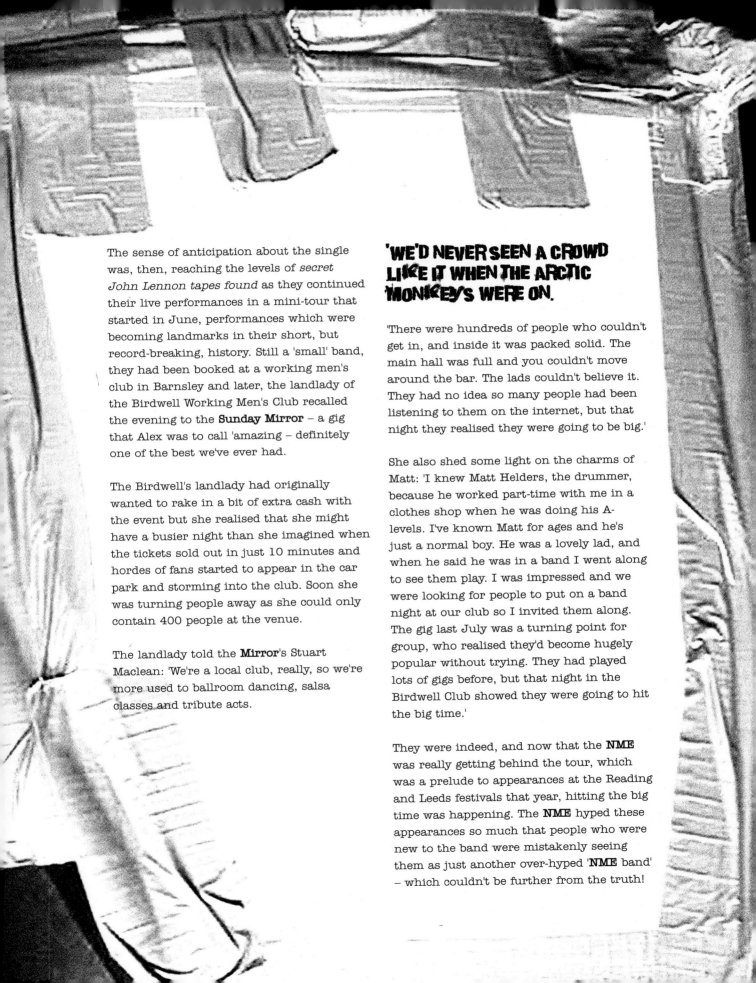

The sense of anticipation about the single was, then, reaching the levels of *secret John Lennon tapes found* as they continued their live performances in a mini-tour that started in June, performances which were becoming landmarks in their short, but record-breaking, history. Still a 'small' band, they had been booked at a working men's club in Barnsley and later, the landlady of the Birdwell Working Men's Club recalled the evening to the **Sunday Mirror** – a gig that Alex was to call 'amazing – definitely one of the best we've ever had.

The Birdwell's landlady had originally wanted to rake in a bit of extra cash with the event but she realised that she might have a busier night than she imagined when the tickets sold out in just 10 minutes and hordes of fans started to appear in the car park and storming into the club. Soon she was turning people away as she could only contain 400 people at the venue.

The landlady told the **Mirror**'s Stuart Maclean: 'We're a local club, really, so we're more used to ballroom dancing, salsa classes and tribute acts.

'WE'D NEVER SEEN A CROWD LIKE IT WHEN THE ARCTIC MONKEYS WERE ON.

'There were hundreds of people who couldn't get in, and inside it was packed solid. The main hall was full and you couldn't move around the bar. The lads couldn't believe it. They had no idea so many people had been listening to them on the internet, but that night they realised they were going to be big.'

She also shed some light on the charms of Matt: 'I knew Matt Helders, the drummer, because he worked part-time with me in a clothes shop when he was doing his A-levels. I've known Matt for ages and he's just a normal boy. He was a lovely lad, and when he said he was in a band I went along to see them play. I was impressed and we were looking for people to put on a band night at our club so I invited them along. The gig last July was a turning point for group, who realised they'd become hugely popular without trying. They had played lots of gigs before, but that night in the Birdwell Club showed they were going to hit the big time.'

They were indeed, and now that the **NME** was really getting behind the tour, which was a prelude to appearances at the Reading and Leeds festivals that year, hitting the big time was happening. The **NME** hyped these appearances so much that people who were new to the band were mistakenly seeing them as just another over-hyped '**NME** band' – which couldn't be further from the truth!

And despite all the hype, Reading and Leeds both had a 'Birdwell', woefully underestimating the number of people that would want to see the Monkeys and placing them in unsuitable slots – at Reading, the band and their followers were packed into a tent which simply couldn't contain them and the real audience spilled out 20 feet beyond the tent. They were the talk of both festivals, even though they were way down the bill on both occasions. At Reading, they were on in the afternoon, but by 11 a.m. their fans were laying siege to the Carling stage.

BY THE AFTERNOON, THERE WAS A 'MON—KEYS, MON—KEYS' CHANT RINGING ROUND THE TENT AND THE CROWD WERE BERSERK BY THE TIME THE BAND WERE WALKING ON TO THE STAGE.

Time restrictions meant that they blazed through the songs at three times the rate in an effort to cram everything in – but, if anything, it made the crowdsurfers even more enthusiastic. Perhaps Reading was the performance where the legend was not born, but enshrined. It was prophetic that when Alex had walked on, he had said with a warranted swagger: 'Don't believe the hype, Reading. They haven't hyped us up enough yet!'

Actually this was when the **NME** and others really started hyping the band. The **NME** giving them the award of Best New Band for their performance at Reading, asking that loaded question: 'Were You There?' and saying that 'the only thing that matters is being here to witness the point when The People forged their own superstar from a scrawny kid from Sheffield.'

But did the superstars have a great single in them? Not only that, they had a Number One single in 'I Bet You Look Good On The Dancefloor', the fiery and angst-ridden alternative dancefloor stomp. Fans of the Monkeys' favourites, The Jam, fondly recall the sense of pride (and disbelief) when two of their singles 'Going Underground' and 'Town Called Malice' entered the charts at number one. Thus, the Monkeys were emulating their heroes with their first single – an incredible achievement, which they celebrated at their local with friends and family while listening on the radio to the announcement.

In deference to the age of the internet and Ipods, the **NME** christened the song Track Of The Week and exhorted their readers to forget about the Libertines:

'FEAR NOT LIB FANS, FOR ITS TIME TO INVEST YOURSELF IN ARCTIC MONKEYS. WE GUARANTEE THEY'LL PAY YOU BACK IN SPADES.'

And rather like the 'Number One' night at the pub, the Monkeys were looking after their own fans with a special secret gig that brought chaos to the streets of Sheffield. Over 200 fans queued for the 80 tickets to see the band at the Grapes, the scene of their first triumph and some fans were offered ten times the price of their tickets. During the ticket rush, Matt's mum handed out cakes and chocolate to fans – one of the calmer moments in an event that rivalled a U2 concert for live hysteria.

The next live stop for the band was the Astoria in October, a gig timed by Domino to coincide with the release of the single. This was their first major-league venue, capable of holding 2000 people at a push – the official capacity was 1,500 but it was 2,000 or more on the night. Tickets for the gig were being exchanged for over a £100 but, as reports showed, the ardour of the fans had been underestimated yet again.

In **The Independent**, Alexis Loundras wrote: 'The excitement outside the Astoria is of the kind reserved for rock legends. Inside, the floor is a rippling mass of anticipation as the packed crowd surges towards the stage long before the band come on. When they do, it's mayhem.'

Loundras also homed in on the growing charisma of Alex whom the crowd were devoted to, instantly stopping any misbehaviour once he said the word. 2,000 fans sang along with Alex, to the amazement of the assembled press, who still couldn't believe that this band had yet to release a single. Asked about the hysteria later that night, a cautious Alex simply and rather disarmingly said:

'I'M SURE ONE DAY IT WILL COME BACK AND BITE US IN THE ARSE.'

But for now the Monkeys had conquered London – without even really trying. In the **Evening Standard**, their music critic John Aizelwood was agog at what he had just seen: '...when I saw them at a triumphant, jampacked Astoria show, twice upgraded from smaller venues, the crowd knew every word to every song. They were thrilling.'

In fact, it was all so raucous and loud that Andy had a nosebleed as they started one song and Alex only got to sing four words of 'When The Sun Comes Down' before the crowd took over. Such was the confidence of the band now that they played their best-known songs in the first five minutes! By all account, this was perhaps one of the best gigs to have seen them play.

But the Monkeys weren't only playing gigs in October. They finally set about putting down tracks for the hugely anticipated debut album. There was no title as yet and they were of course, going back to the demos that had been circulating already. There were also some new tracks to look forward to.

'The album's going to be made up of a few of the old demos,' said Alex. 'A few of the

tunes that everyone knows live. It wouldn't be fair to leave them off this album. There's also a few newer ones that haven't been played live to give it balance.'

They secreted themselves in a Lincolnshire studio and secured the services of Jim Abbiss, a respected producer who had already worked with Kasabian, The Music and DJ Shadow. Of course, there was no trouble about working on arrangements as the band had been playing most of them live or in rehearsal non-stop – Abbiss just had to guide them about the sound of the songs which were, naturally enough, intended to be finished at high speed. They were keen to capture some of the excitement of the live shows with everything recorded live.

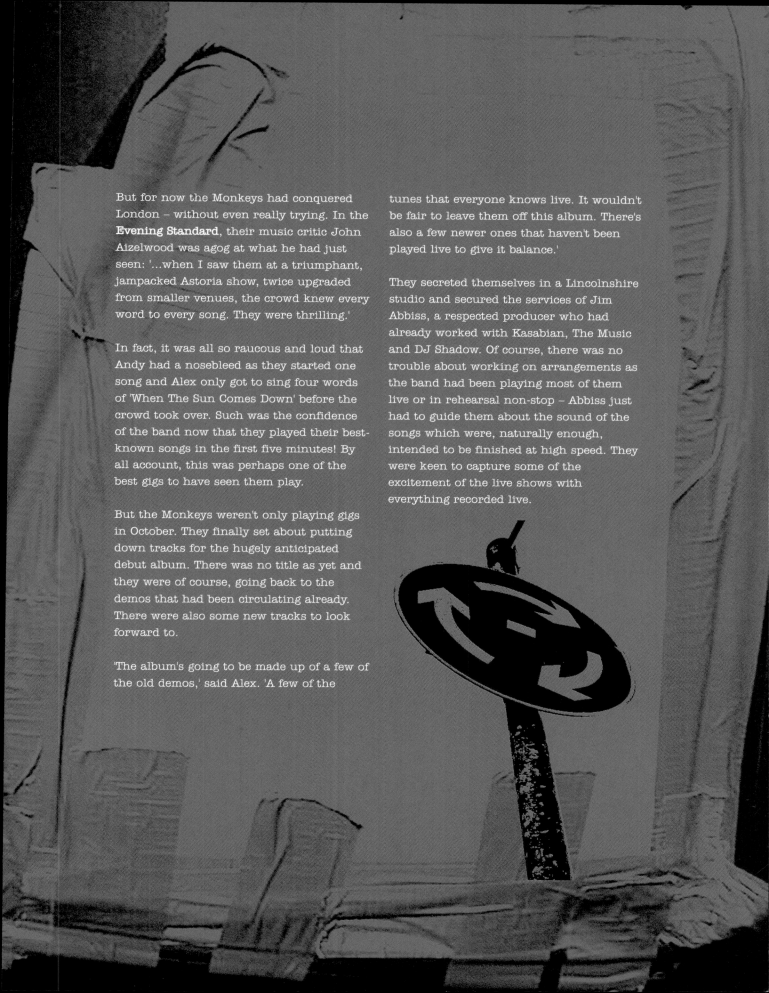

Actually, it had to be recorded quickly because the band were thinking of going out live again pretty soon – first a short UK tour, then America. America is a momentous step for any UK band and, arguably, far more for the Monkeys because their popularity came largely from their grass-roots followinig. They knew they could just corpse without their hardcore fans. Alex put what concerned them all: 'It's going to be weird because we're starting again there. We're going to go out there and see what they think.'

On all their minds, as well, was that if they were ignored in the US, it could backfire on their UK rep. Yet, as Liam said of them, 'I dunno about their music but the one thing I like about the Artic Monkeys is they don't give a monkeys.'

They weren't even fazed by the news that bootleggers were selling some of the freely available music that the Monkeys had already made. Some bootleggers had put all the original demos onto a CD and were selling them as unofficial 'Monkeys albums'. The band and Domino issued a warning, but the market was on a Pamplona run: it emerged that copies of their debut EP were selling for £100 a pop.

The **NME** Cool List, published at the end of every year, is usually the most reliable barometer for what is most popular in young 'indie' music. The usual thing that happens is that an artist climbs up (or down) a few places each year: it's pretty rare for someone to land in the higher reaches out of nowhere. But this is exactly what happened with Alex, straight in at number one – a sure sign of the frantically-paced success of the band. The list is usually full of glamour, too, and the **NME** delighted in the fact that Alex was so ordinary ('he even sounds like he should be packing your bags at Asda for you'); they also seemed delighted with the fact that he was, presumably, supremely unbothered about the whole thing – 'not wanting to be cool makes you even more nipple-stiffeningly credible than you were before'.

In order to look like its making the running on what's happening next, our rock bible uses cringe like 'nipple-stiffeningly credible'.

There were all kinds of indications of the speed of the band's ascent detectable now. One sign was an interview with Noel Gallagher, who is now commonly known as the 'Godfather of Indie'; he is someone who had been around the block of course, but is he also well known for being meticulous about clocking the new talent. He turns up at all manner of local gigs, not so much to size up the competition as lift any ideas that could work for Oasis. His first recorded comment about the Monkeys, on Radio One, was that they had a 'shit name' but it turned out that he was still to hear any of their music – he wasn't even sure if they had an album out.

One person who had made a point of finding more out about them was Ian Brown, one of the people behind the hottest debut albums of all time, **The Stone Roses**. An original punk rocker, he saw the same spirit in the Monkeys after being introduced to them by his 15-year-old niece who had seen them four times already. 'I like the Arctic Monkeys because they've got an edge that I think has been missing from bands for five or ten years,' he said, 'There's not a lot of energy in bands these days. Arctic Monkeys have got that energy. And I love the way they are northern. You don't hear many good northern voices on records, so it's nice to hear a northern voice there.'

These were all astute points. Aside from the pack of bands like the Libertines or Razorlight, the indie bands that predominated British music were either American imports aiming at the youth end of the market – or bands like Coldplay or Keane usually playing medium tempo, angsty music (often known as 'Weep Pop' or 'music to wet your bed to'), which was, in reality, better suited for thirtysomethings or even older (haven't they got a grave to go to?). Suddenly, though, here was a young testosteronic band with a fanbase that was far younger than any drawn to the aforementioned groups. This really was music for disaffected teenagers (and by definition teenagers should be disaffected), especially those on an ASBOS or tagged or banged up.

Another icon of the time was the Libertines' Pete Doherty. In the controversy that surrounded the Monkeys, somebody had already ventured to christen them the 'Northern Libertines', highlighting how similar the Monkeys' close relationship with their audience, via concerts and the internet, was to the Libertines' first concerts at people's houses and the like, borrowing guitar strings from audience members and mingling with them freely.

But, of course, Doherty had become mired in being an A-list celebrity with an A-list celebrity girlfriend and a Class A drug problem – and, after he exploited all his friends to feed his habit, he was dumped by his crew and, later, his girlfriend. He responded by hastily launching Babyshambles, which may have marginalised the Doherty-less Libertines, but it fell a long way short of their musicianship. Babyshambles staggered on mainly on the back of Doherty's busts and court appearances, but really as just another loser in the celebrity mosh pit. It was now the Arctic Monkeys, more than anyone else, who represented the long-overdue antidote to celebrity culture.

THESE WERE SPOTTY KIDS FROM SHEFFIELD WHO STILL LIVED AT THEIR PARENTS' HOUSES WHO WANTED NOTHING TO DO WITH TV, HEAT OR THE CULT OF CELEBRITY.

And, amazingly, there were people out there – and plenty of them – that loved them for it.

But this wasn't the only reason that the mass media had become intrigued by the success of the Arctic Monkeys. For the last few years, all the papers and TV had been reporting the demise of the record industry – and the figures for CD sales looked like they were going to confirm it. It was clear that a lot of the Monkeys' audience already had their music – they were singing along to easy enough. But what was really strange was that it really looked like they were going to buy the second single in their droves as well.

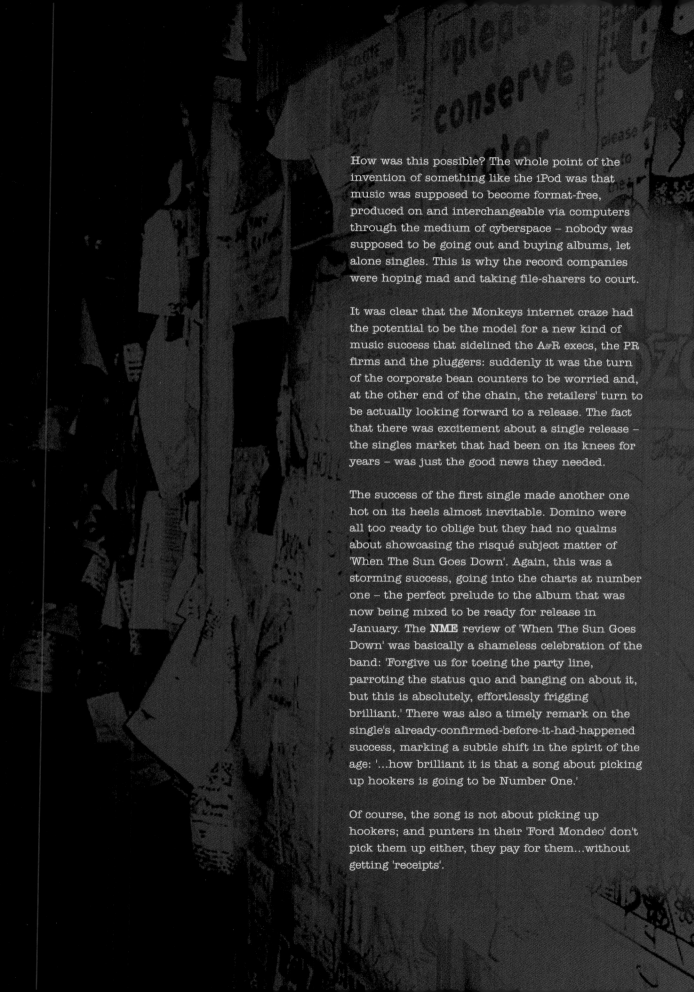

How was this possible? The whole point of the invention of something like the iPod was that music was supposed to become format-free, produced on and interchangeable via computers through the medium of cyberspace – nobody was supposed to be going out and buying albums, let alone singles. This is why the record companies were hoping mad and taking file-sharers to court.

It was clear that the Monkeys internet craze had the potential to be the model for a new kind of music success that sidelined the A&R execs, the PR firms and the pluggers: suddenly it was the turn of the corporate bean counters to be worried and, at the other end of the chain, the retailers' turn to be actually looking forward to a release. The fact that there was excitement about a single release – the singles market that had been on its knees for years – was just the good news they needed.

The success of the first single made another one hot on its heels almost inevitable. Domino were all too ready to oblige but they had no qualms about showcasing the risqué subject matter of 'When The Sun Goes Down'. Again, this was a storming success, going into the charts at number one – the perfect prelude to the album that was now being mixed to be ready for release in January. The **NME** review of 'When The Sun Goes Down' was basically a shameless celebration of the band: 'Forgive us for toeing the party line, parroting the status quo and banging on about it, but this is absolutely, effortlessly frigging brilliant.' There was also a timely remark on the single's already-confirmed-before-it-had-happened success, marking a subtle shift in the spirit of the age: '...how brilliant it is that a song about picking up hookers is going to be Number One.'

Of course, the song is not about picking up hookers; and punters in their 'Ford Mondeo' don't pick them up either, they pay for them...without getting 'receipts'.

People were now witnessing something that they thought they had seen the last of. There had plenty of people who had had consecutive number ones recently but the sales figures for them had become ludicrously low, making the prestige of being Number One less and less important. The fans of the Monkeys – who had all the music anyway – had made buying the official product a badge of honour, an article of faith showing their loyalty to the band. In the end, 'When The Sun Goes Down', a song that had originally been called 'Scummy' sold 38,922 copies in the first week alone. It made the projected sales for the album almost impossible to predict and pre-orders were already going through the roof.

In the end, something had to give such was the furore about the album now. In the second week in January, Domino decided to bring forward the release of the album. Laurence Bell said: 'People are always putting albums back so we thought it would be fun to bring one forward. The manufacturing went quicker than expected and the thinking was that the albums are going to do more good if they are in the shops rather than sat in the Domino warehouse for an extra week.' It was sound thinking in many ways and as for the band, given their close relationship to the audience and loyalty to the small-scale operation of Domino, one could only imagine them applauding it. In fact, Laurence Bell couldn't help crowing about it too: 'part of the fun of being an independent label is that we can change our minds if we like. We're not burdened by rigid corporate structure.'

The album, called **Whatever People Say I Am, That's What I'm Not** was
thus unveiled in mid-January 2006. The title was taken from
dialogue used in the kitchen sink film of the Alan Sillitoe novel.
Saturday Night and Sunday Morning – which would also have been a
great title for the album – had those immortal lines spoken defiantly
by Albert Finney – 'Whatever people say I am, that's what I am not.
Because they don't know a bloody thing about me.'

The cover was a brilliant image too, echoing some of the abrasive,
moody, 'fuck 'em and leave 'em' image of Albert Finney in the film
('All I want is a good time. The rest is propaganda').

Long-time friend of the band Clive McClure is seen drawing on a fag
in a sweaty, smokey northern club. It's a grainy, grimy shot but
sharply reflects the atmosphere of the songs and Alex's lyrics.

The **NME** could do little else than bring forward their review of the album, and they did so with a clear championing of Alex as the major young songwriter of the age, turning their back on a former favourite: '...forget the flowery fantasies cooked up by Dickensian Doherty – these are tales of the scum-ridden streets as they are in 2006, not 1906.' They went even further by placing the band in grand company, calling **Whatever...** 'a stripped-down punk rock record with every touchstone of Great British Music Covered: the Britishness of the Kinks, the melodic nous of the Beatles, the sneer of Sex Pistols, the wit of the Smiths, the groove of the Stone Roses, the anthems of Oasis, the clatter of the Libertine...' Needless to say, the **NME** gave it a ten.

The four page feature in the **NME** that followed, as they were announced on the **NME** Shockwaves Awards show, was another part of the snowball. It emerged that the band were already making their second album but trying, if anything, to dispel the aura that had built up around them, with their name bandied about in the unlikeliest circles. Alex said: 'Internet Masterminds Top The Charts!' and all this shit. It were in, like, **The Economist** or something like that and reading all the papers the next day, it said how we used to fucking hold live chats and that.' To which Matt retorted: **'I DIDN'T EVEN KNOW HOW TO GET ON TO OUR FORUM.'**

At the end of January, the **NME**'s excitement about the album bubbled over so much that they hauled in Alex to go through the album track by track just before its release – a compliment normally reserved for the biggest bands in the country, and normally done after the album has been released. This was happening after having already offered an exclusive preview of the album. His comments on the by now hugely familiar songs were illuminating and reliably straightforward and often an insight into the way the Monkeys had been in their humdrum early days.

'Riot Van', for instance, was the one song that seemed to have a 'history' in that it was 'set' in a time when the band were all about 14 and they were clearly on the threshold of either doing something useful with their lives – or becoming ne'er-do-wells. Alex still felt that he had to defend themselves from being 'ASBO' types: 'It's all about when we used to hang about our end and the things we saw. We were never really bad lads, we just used to have a laugh. I think Helders described it best when he said "Just 'cos you'd hang around near people who might burgle house or summat it didn't mean *you* had to".'

His comment on 'Fake Tales From San Francisco' demonstrated how far they had in such a short space of time, having first been aired in the summer of 2004. 'We just started playing what seemed like a lot of gigs – sometimes we'd go mad and play two a week. The gigs were usually four band or sometimes more, no-one in the crowd except a few mates or girlfriends who all left as soon as they could.'

The same could be said of 'Perhaps Vampires Is A Bit Strong But' written when they were starting to play outside Sheffield. 'You get expenses covered most of the time but that was all – you never made a profit or anything like that.

'When you talked to people about it however, it was somewhat frowned upon and perhaps sniggered at that we were playing for free. Everyone's an expert about this band lark and it seemed like a joke to a lot of people.

'WHILE THEY'D WISH US ALL THE BEST I THINK BEHIND OUR BACKS THEY WERE REALLY CONVINCED THAT WE WERE JUST WASTING OUR TIME.'

Once the album was out there, no one could ever again say the band had been wasting their time or that the success of the singles was a fluke. The album stunned everyone: it became the fastest selling debut album in chart history, selling 363,735 copies in the first week. This destroyed the previous record of 306,631 copies held by Hear'say with **Popstars**, and is likely to be even higher once online downloads of the album are added. The record's first day sales alone – 118,501 copies – made it the fastest selling debut rock album, enough to secure the Number One chart position. Now, the record business would have to get used to the Monkeys – they were here to stay, it seemed.

FIVE

It was more than enough to have those people from the labels that had tried unsuccessfully to sign the band, gnawing at their knuckles with frustration. Alex now revealed actually how overbearing and short-sighted they had been. 'Before the hysteria started,' he said, 'labels would say "I like you, but I'm not sure about this bit, and that song could do with this changing..." and we never listened. And once it all kicked off we didn't even worry about it anymore. In London, the kids were watching the band and the record company were at the back watching the kids watching the band.'

It also has to be remembered here that the band had done all this with minimal TV coverage too. Bands like Hear'say relentlessly promote on all media – the Monkeys had already vehemently refused to do **Top Of The Pops**. This was a promise that they had made when they were talking in interviews about not doing any 'bollocks'. The only TV that they had done was **Popworld E4 Music** and **Later with Jools Holland**. On 12 November 2005, the Monkeys' Liverpool gig was featured on MTV2's **Gonzo on Tour**; in fact, the channel rushed the footage onto the channel two weeks prior to the rest of the **Gonzo On Tour**, the week they hit number one, and proceeded to repeat the footage several times a day.

The touring seemed to show no signs of abating too and, following the pretty favourable reaction to their first small USA gigs a major tour was announced for the States in March 2006. The band are due to play headlining gigs in San Francisco, Los Angeles, Chicago, Toronto, Montreal, Boston, New York, Philadelphia and Washington, amongst others. In addition to these, the band will be the opening act for none other than Oasis at the 15,000-capacity Air Canada Centre in Toronto.

After that, there is another UK tour and there seems to be no sign of the excitement about them as a live draw slowing down. At the end of January 2006, James 'the Sherrif' announced details of the Monkeys' UK tour in April 2006. The tour, beginning on 13 April in Nottingham, consists of 12 gigs around the UK and culminates on 27 April at Brixton Academy in London. Advanced tickets to all 12 shows were made available on the Monkeys' web-site at 6pm that night, and sold out within 15 minutes.

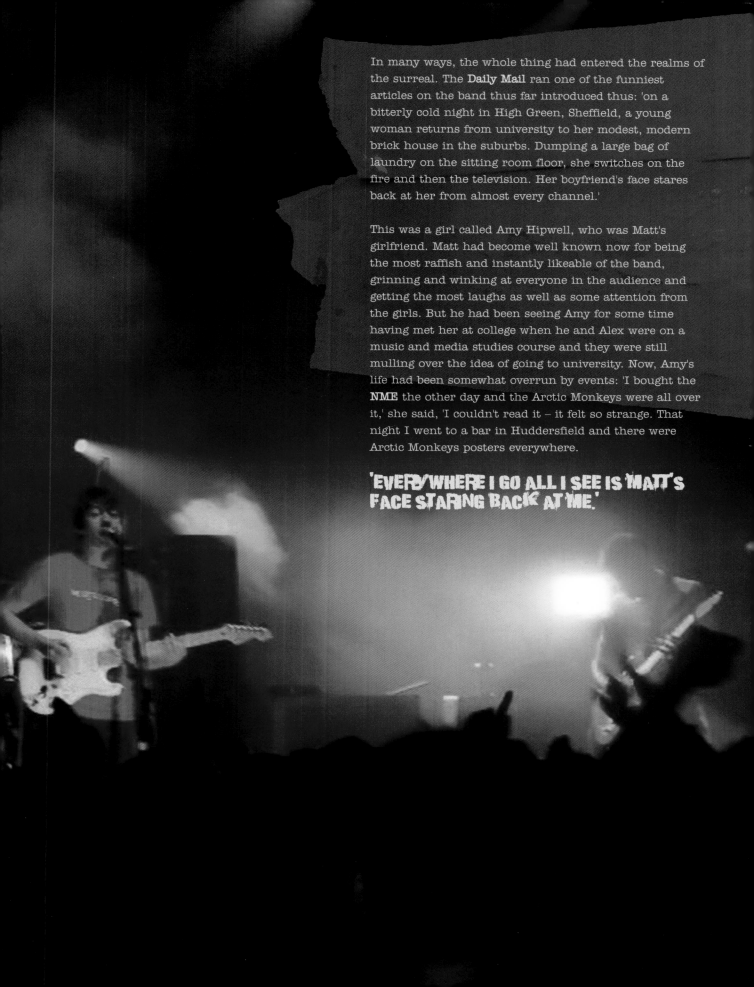

In many ways, the whole thing had entered the realms of the surreal. The **Daily Mail** ran one of the funniest articles on the band thus far introduced thus: 'on a bitterly cold night in High Green, Sheffield, a young woman returns from university to her modest, modern brick house in the suburbs. Dumping a large bag of laundry on the sitting room floor, she switches on the fire and then the television. Her boyfriend's face stares back at her from almost every channel.'

This was a girl called Amy Hipwell, who was Matt's girlfriend. Matt had become well known now for being the most raffish and instantly likeable of the band, grinning and winking at everyone in the audience and getting the most laughs as well as some attention from the girls. But he had been seeing Amy for some time having met her at college when he and Alex were on a music and media studies course and they were still mulling over the idea of going to university. Now, Amy's life had been somewhat overrun by events: 'I bought the **NME** the other day and the Arctic Monkeys were all over it,' she said, 'I couldn't read it – it felt so strange. That night I went to a bar in Huddersfield and there were Arctic Monkeys posters everywhere.

'EVERYWHERE I GO ALL I SEE IS MATT'S FACE STARING BACK AT ME.'

The **Daily Mail** was reporting in true kitchen-sink style, looking at these lives and careers up north as if they were looking at them for the first time. Amy was asked about what her and Matt did: '...mostly we go out for meals and the cinema and he comes to stay in Huddersfield.' And Amy's mother, Angela, works as a care assistant while her father is a caretaker whose passion is metal detecting.'

They also tracked down another local landlady who knew the band and who hadn't given a paper her penny's worth so far. This was Jayne Ridal, the landlady of their local, The Packhorse, in High Green. She was recalling the night when the band had their first number one single as if they were the Beatles or something. 'When it got close to seven o' clock,' she said, 'one of the lads came over and asked whether it would be OK to put on the radio to see where they would come in the chart. When they were No 1, the whole pub went mad.'

Next, they made a stop at Jamie's old school, Ecclestone High School, where they were proud of his success – even though not many people could remember which one he was. 'Jamie is a cracking lad,' said head of music Dave Corker. 'But having had chats in the staff room, hardly anybody can say anything about him. He was a quiet lad who blended in with the crowd.'

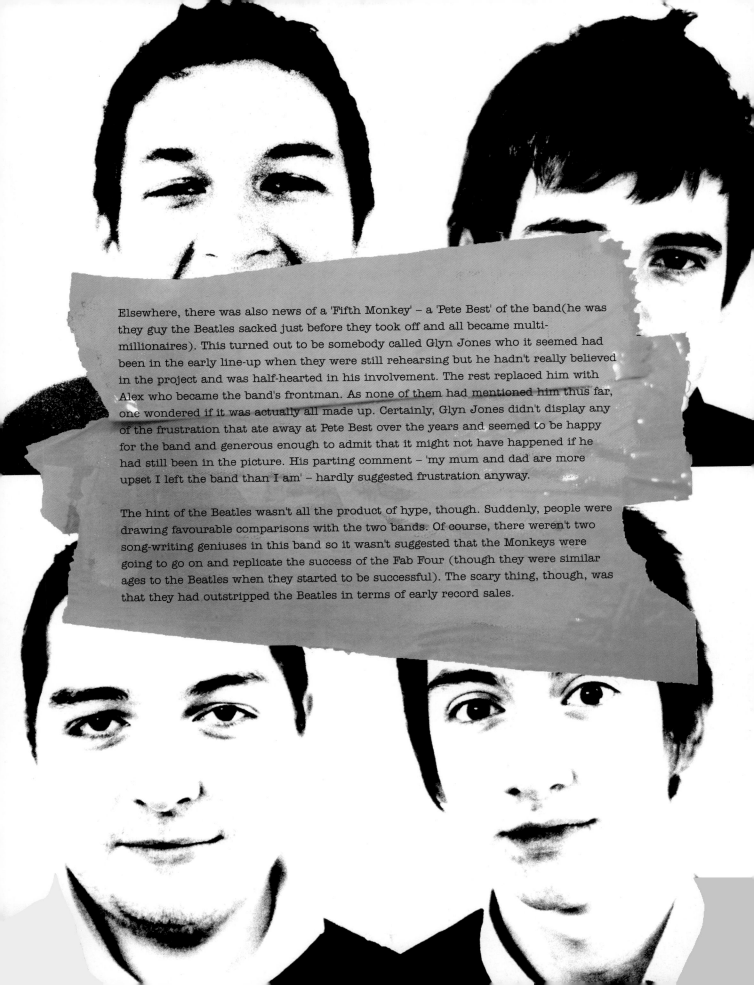

Elsewhere, there was also news of a 'Fifth Monkey' – a 'Pete Best' of the band(he was they guy the Beatles sacked just before they took off and all became multi-millionaires). This turned out to be somebody called Glyn Jones who it seemed had been in the early line-up when they were still rehearsing but he hadn't really believed in the project and was half-hearted in his involvement. The rest replaced him with Alex who became the band's frontman. As none of them had mentioned him thus far, one wondered if it was actually all made up. Certainly, Glyn Jones didn't display any of the frustration that ate away at Pete Best over the years and seemed to be happy for the band and generous enough to admit that it might not have happened if he had still been in the picture. His parting comment – 'my mum and dad are more upset I left the band than I am' – hardly suggested frustration anyway.

The hint of the Beatles wasn't all the product of hype, though. Suddenly, people were drawing favourable comparisons with the two bands. Of course, there weren't two song-writing geniuses in this band so it wasn't suggested that the Monkeys were going to go on and replicate the success of the Fab Four (though they were similar ages to the Beatles when they started to be successful). The scary thing, though, was that they had outstripped the Beatles in terms of early record sales.

The gig at the Astoria, now seeming like it was years back in October 2005, was remarkable because no major league band had ever drawn such a crowd with just one single to their name. And the figures for **Whatever...** were unprecedented. Also, they seemed to invent a new mode of expression in music (something that the Beatles had done on possibly a couple of occasions in their career) that made it all the more exciting. Most of all, it was clear they weren't a flash in the pan band at all and would be with us for a long time to come. Even so, all this attention brought one of the best quotes from Alex who couldn't fail to see the madness of some of the hype: 'As good as we know it is, it's like it'll be built up to such a thing that if it doesn't cure cancer or solve inner city poverty or something it'll be a disaster.'

News in February that the band was actually going to have a film coming out only reminded everyone forcibly of the Beatles again. It turned out that it was only a short film, a scenario based on 'When The Sun Comes Down' and, more than anything, it was an exciting stopgap for fans who would be impatiently waiting for the second album (which was still, apparently, being worked on) and any gash singles.

But the Beatles comparisons were, if anything, becoming a bit of cliché. **The Independent** reported on the band in a way that was highly reverential, seeing them, like the Beatles, worthy of serious cultural comment from a host of luminaries in the arts, a couple of whom just couldn't stop themselves from mentioning the Beatles themselves. Fittingly, these included Alan Sillittoe who pronounced himself flattered (in a way) that the band had used one of his novels for inspiration. He also found reasons for actually liking them: 'I was more surprised than flattered I suppose when they took the title of the album from my book **Saturday Night and Sunday Morning**. I'm mainly a big jazz and classical fan, not really into pop at all.

'I MUST SAY IT IS MARVELLOUS. I REALLY LIKE IT AND IT'S GOT ME DANCING AROUND THE ROOM.

'I'm from Nottingham, which is a very similar place to Sheffield and I can recognise their accents and their background. I think that reflecting their background is what helps lift them above other groups. IF YOU LOCALISE WITH SUFFICIENT INTEGRITY, YOU ACHIEVE UNIVERSALITY.

'The sheer life and energy that they convey is a very good thing in this rather dead and politically correct society that we live in. They seem to have that connection to what real people think and want.'

Next was an artist, Stella Vine: 'I first heard of them six months ago, and have been playing the album all weekend. I bought **NME** for the first time in about two years this weekend, to see if there were pictures of the band. I am in the process of doing a painting of the band. The lyrics reminded me of the Beatles because they are profound truths of existence, but anyone can tap in and relate to them. They are poetic, and very English sounding, very real.' (Yes, Stella! Keep up the visits to your therapist.)

The paper even tracked down the Monkey's local MP, Clive Betts: 'I have to say I like this very much. I'm quite impressed, in fact. They seem to be talking in language that young people will respond too. I think it is a great thing for Sheffield because although we have a history of producing good bands, in the past we have often been overshadowed by Liverpool and Manchester.'

The Liverpool poet, Roger 'the doggerel' McGough, mentioning Alex's lyrical inspiration was less impressed: 'They write John Cooper Clarke, Morrissey, northern gritty lyrics that appeal to the market and their peers. Good luck to them. What they are writing is song lyrics, which is a different skill than writing poetry, because you are writing with music in your head.

MY 15—YEAR—OLD DAUGHTER LIKES THEM, BUT I DON'T QUITE UNDERSTAND THE FUSS TO DO WITH THE LYRICS... YET.'

(Cooper Clarke will explain Roger.)

The rest of the contributors which ran from music industry people to a fellow musician like Dion Chapman were all generally positive, but it was left to style guru Peter 'The Sloane Ranger' York to put the limp wrist in:

'I like the idea of them more than the sound of them. I'm just an airhead metropolitanist. I like the idea of a British slice of life, but this isn't a life that I want a slice of. It's British in the wrong way – I prefer something more poncy myself.

'They are quite enthusiastic, but a bit tedious. Pop is getting so much better in principle, but not necessarily in practice.

'I admire their marketing, and I quite admire their name – it's amusing: but is it really a nice sound? Not very... it's a bit dreary.'
(Dready is a very Peter York word.)

For the most pertinent comment you have to go back to Alan Sillitoe': 'I think that reflecting their background is what helps lift them above other groups – if you localise with sufficient integrity, you achieve universality.'

This goes to the heart of the appeal of the Arctic Monkeys. The majority of artists like the Monkeys, from time immemorial are told, or tell themselves, that they should write about what they know. This is a central tenet of the band – as Alex reminded us:

'WHAT ELSE IS THERE TO WRITE ABOUT?'

If vitality and relevance matter, this is more crucial than ever in early 21st century pop music. For one thing, the manner in which bands are made these days follows a well-worn pattern where, the more money a big record company has (and no one doubts that it will always be dominated by majors), the less they want to take risks like they did in the punk era with bands that had some of the most absurd names imaginable – rather like the Monkeys, in fact.

The market tempts bands to follow the record industry money. Those that adopt the success formula may well make it but, whatever the returns, it will be at the cost of their originality. And when they look back, it will be in the knowledge that they sold out their talent.

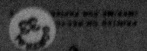

No major label in the eighties would have touched the Smiths until they had been blooded on an indie like Rough Trade and, as we have seen with Oasis, the indies have, if anything, increasingly merged with the majors so that smaller labels take the risks and the majors cash in exactly when it suits them. This has meant that there has been less and less of a chance that unique voices will be heard – and no one believed that anyone could steal in through any gap to reach audiences any more directly than was thought possible.

Nonetheless this is exactly what the Arctic Monkeys have done and done unwittingly, simply by handing over all the spare CDs they had when they were confronted by a small sea of fans at the end of a gig in a club in the North. The internet, which the record industry with its war on file-sharing had thought it had mastered, simply did the rest. Thus, the Monkeys reached an audience writing and singing about what they knew about without any controlling influence from any label, and without any PR makeover.

he simple, unadorned messages and stories that the band
carried were instantly recognised by a youth that had
probably been overfed, not only with dressed-up music of all
kinds, but also celebrity gossip, mindless and violent video
games and bad TV. It was direct communication with youth
certainly on a par with the punk revolution in the seventies,
but this time carried through one band only, not a host of
them and it has never really happened before – even the
Beatles were part of the Merseybeat era.

On a wider level, the ascent of this relentlessly ordinary, but
very talented group is symbolic for the age. In the early 21st
century Britain as a whole is a place that that has become
homogenised as much as its youth. It's long been bemoaned
about the replica high streets across the country with the
same coffee bars, mobile phone retailers and same banks –

IF THE PUNKS WERE BORED AND NEEDED AN OUTLET IN THE STREETS OF THE SEVENTIES, HOW BORED MUST TODAY'S YOUTH BE.

The question of identity is pretty much paramount in a world that is rapidly losing it, and it's more crucial than ever for today's youth. The Arctic Monkeys phenom has allowed their fans to feel that they have an identity in common with a band that, for once, is like them. Alex Turner writes about standing on street corners looking at binge drinkers or going to clubs hating bands and ogling girls: Chris Martin of Coldplay writes love songs to his Hollywood actress wife – given the choice between the two, which one would the youth of today choose?

Yet the band does also cross over to the last generations, many of whom remember the heady days of punk or the days of the Smiths. It's unquestioned that this is a highly skilled pop band and, in Alex Turner, despite his tender years, they have a sophisticated songwriter and lyricist. The big question is if they can sustain these levels of success and, perhaps more intriguingly, carry it over into other markets, especially the States. The groundswell of reaction to the Monkeys' music does bear comparison with the US embrace of Nirvana over a decade ago. The bleak messages of Kurt Cobain struck a chord on both sides of the Atlantic then too – and there's no reason why Alex Turner's similarly bleak, but less tortured songs shouldn't carry over.

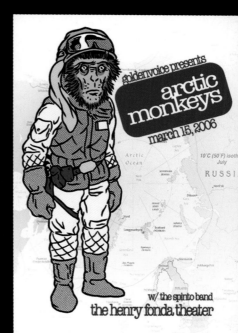

WHEN THE SUN GOES DOWN

Who's that girl there?
I wonder what went wrong
So that she had to roam the streets
She dunt do major credit cards
I doubt she does receipts
It's all not quite legitimate

And what a scummy man
Just give him half a chance
I bet he'll rob you if he can
Can see it in his eyes,
That he's got a driving ban
Amongst some other offences

And I've seen him with girls of the night
And he told Roxanne to put on her red light
Its all infected but he'll be alright
Cause he's a scumbag, don't you know
I said he's a scumbag, don't you know!...

Arctic are clearly the new kids on the indie block and, especially with Alex's lyrics, they are definitely no fluke. They came up on the outside without anyone except their fans even watching, never mind noticing, and like all outsiders that beat the odds they are now being billed as unbeatable.... well, as we know, the new Beatles.

But as musicians they are still technically very limited and in an era when most bands have at least one player in the Jimmie Hendrix league. Takes Strokes lead guitar Nick Valensi – he was playing in bands at the age of 11! And composition tends to run in tandem with musicianship. To stay the course the Arctic Monkeys are going to need more than Alex's lyricism.

As Tim de Lisle noted tellingly in the **Mail on Sunday:** Alex 'combines a streetwise brain with the ability, too often educated out of bright kids, to write in pictures. RUDE, EXUBERANT AND RELENTLESSLY VIVID, HE IS HOGARTH IN A HOODIE. THE MUSIC CAN'T ALWAYS KEEP UP. THERE'S PLENTY OF FIERCE ENERGY, BUT NOT MUCH INSPIRATION.'

OK, they can import some – like a hotshot keyboard man to fill out the sound and develop the arrangements, but this will change the mix and chemistry of the group. The ideal solution, of course, is they really work at their respective techniques. Perhaps their biggest asset is their realism. Alex commented at the end of 2005: 'We're not professionals...the sooner people realise that, the better.' Well, maybe, but there is a lot of fan power willing them on to become professionals.

Nonetheless, Tim de Lisle, who is one of the more perceptive journos on pop music, sees the Monkeys as 'compelling...abrasive and exceptional' and too talented not to rise to the challenge ahead of them. There is an old saying in rock music: 'If you can get girls and lads on to the dancefloor at the same time then the chances are you're going to be big.' By that standard, even if they don't get any better, Artic Monkeys will get bigger. But, like Tim de Lisle, you feel that they will get better too.

BUT THESE GUY'S STILL LIVE WITH THEIR PARENTS IN SHEFFIELD!

What happens when the success really rolls over them. Will it go to their head? Of course, it will. In different ways success goes to the head of everyone who gets a taste of it.

And they haven't yet tasted those knickerless Chelsea girls, who boarded at Bendenden, moonlight on the catwalk, and chop out elephant lines of uncut charlie with their platinum AmEx quicker than most of us can key in the pin number of our debit card. At the moment, the band just pass round a joint and give the local groupies their bragging rights but nothing is surer than that this will all change... You don't think so? Ask Liam and Noel.

They are young, success has happened fast, and there are four of them. In their different ways they will all, if they are to keep the show on the road, have to ride out the temptations, the attention, the drugs, the women, the high life. Most successful groups make it when they are older and don't get there quite so quick. The lure of excess will be that much stronger for the Monkeys. Curiously enough not many groups actually succumb completely, but the fall out rate among individuals members makes up for it. How could it be otherwise?

IT WON'T BE EASY FOR THE FOUR MONKEY'S TO JUST SAY YES ...IN MODERATION. ONE THING'S FOR SURE, THEY AIN'T GONNA JUST SAY NO.

Yet, fellow-Sheffield rock'n'roller Jarvis Cocker believes that the Monkeys have got what it takes to rise above the hype and the temptations. Of course, his judgement is compromised by the way he celebrates the band doing with what he signally failed to do: putting two fingers up to the record corporate industry – which largely dictates chart success – and getting away with it.

'I think they're very important,' Cocker says, 'because they've done it without trying. The only reason people have got into it (the music) is because they've listened to it and they like it, so it's something real. I guess all the music industry will probably think 'how can we emulate that or what can we do?" I think there's nothing they can do about it because it's something that has happened naturally, there's no way to apply spin doctorism to it.' He is confident that that their strong ties to what they sing about will keep them on track.

Bill Robinson, who is a DJ and sometime rock'n'roller, is equally sure: 'Can they last? That is the big problem, because we have a climate in which there is a voracious appetite for new music, caused by things like having weekly music papers and Radio One. By the second album for a lot of bands, critics start saying "Oh, they are not that good anyway" and people suddenly don't want to know. It takes an exceptional band to get past that point.

'Everyone said the Beatles were just disposable pop and no-one would remember them... I think kids who are now 15 or 16 and getting into the Arctic Monkeys will be playing their music in 20 years time and they will look back to this era and say to each other *Those were the days...*'

In March 2006 the band will go on their first long North American tour, headlining gigs in San Francisco, Los Angeles, Chicago, Toronto, Montreal, Boston, New York, Philadelphia and Washington, amongst others. In addition to these, the band will be the opening act for an Oasis show at the 15,000-capacity Air Canada Centre in Toronto.

They always look up to Oasis. Matt commented: 'Its a band we've always been into. Oasis has always been there, ever since we were young and growing up. Not necessarily their newer stuff, but I'll always pick up their first album and their second album and listen to them.'

After that they return to the UK to begin a tour on 13 April at Nottingham, which consists of 12 gigs around the UK and culminates on 27 April at Brixton Academy in London. All the gigs are sold out. Then will come the second album...

Crunch time? Maybe. But as Alex says whatever the future, they've already made an indelible mark where it counts:

'People already proper care about the music, before its even finished. **YOU CAN SEE IT IN THEIR EYES AND NOBODY CAN TAKE THAT AWAY FROM YOU.**

'I guess it can still get bigger, though. Instead of hundreds of people singing the words, it could be thousands. **'DOES THAT FEEL ANY DIFFERENT, I WONDER'**